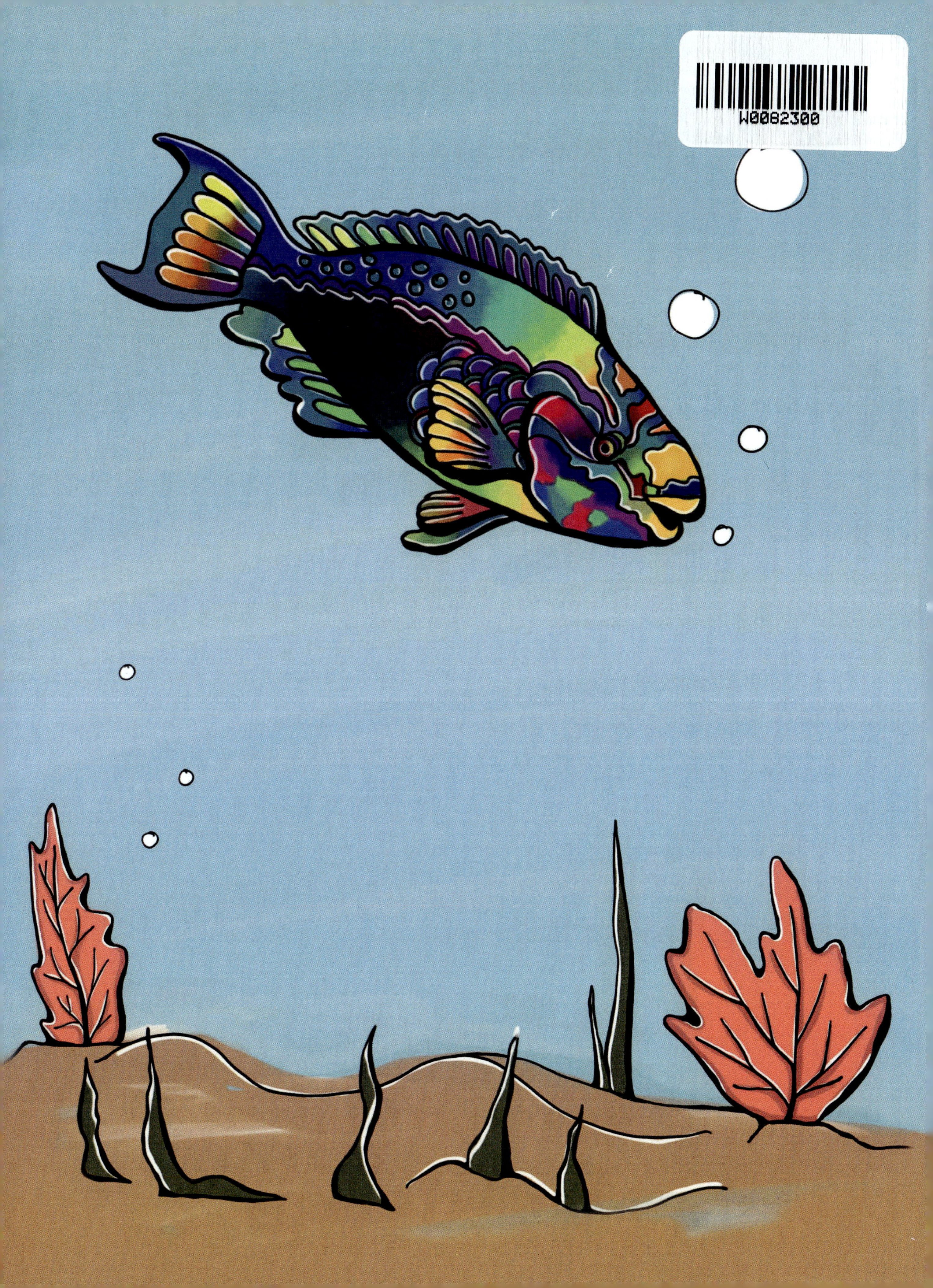

Steven's Funny Fish, A Children's Story

Story by Ronald Semmann; Illustration and Layout by Abbigail Semmann

ISBN 978-1-09833-209-9

Printed in the United States of America

Woodgrove Meadows Press

Steven's Funny Fish

Story by Ronald Semmann

Illustration by Abbigail Semmann

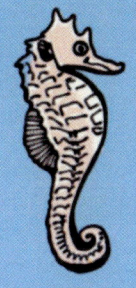

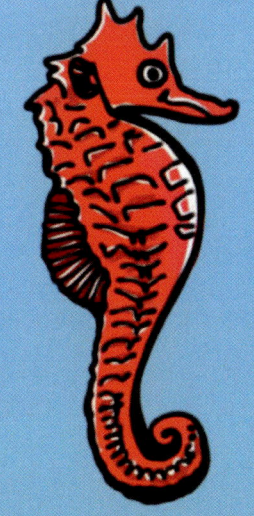

Dedicated to Steven Jay Semmann

On a rainy Sunday in May, Grandfather came
to Steven's house. Steven always enjoyed
Grandfather's visits, and Grandfather often
brought a surprise with him.
"I have a nice surprise for you today," Grandfather said.
"I am going to take you to a very special place."
A special place, Steven thought.
What kind of surprise could that be?
Grandfather knew what Steven was thinking.
"I won't tell you now," he said.
"We'll wait until we get there."

1.

CITY AQUARIUM

Steven and Grandfather drove for a long time. They finally stopped in front of a big white building. The building had large white pillars in front. At the top of the pillars there was a sign.

"What does the sign say?" Steven asked.

"It says CITY AQUARIUM," Grandfather answered. "Come, let's go outside."

As they walked up the steep steps leading to the big doors, Steven asked, "What does aquarium mean?"

Grandfather looked down at him. "An aquarium is like a city home for many different kinds of fish. "You'll see when we go inside."

2.

Steven skipped quickly up the steps,
but he had to wait for Grandfather
to pull open one of the heavy doors.
They both walked inside.
It was darker here than in the light outside.

3.

Steven looked around.
He didn't know which way to go first.
On every wall there were large glass
cases filled with water.
He could see fish swimming in every one.
"Let's go closer and take a better look."
Grandfather said. "All the fish are different.
Some are big and some are small."

"What's this one over here?" Steven asked.

He pointed to a strangely shaped fish.

Grandfather looked up at the small sign over the case.

"That is a Turkeyfish," he said. "Look at those big fins.

They almost look like Turkey feathers.

We don't have any of these in..."

But before he could finish had moved on to the next glass case.

"What is this one?" Steven asked.
"That's a parrotfish," Grandfather answered.
"His mouth is shaped like a..." But again, before he finished,
Steven was looking at the next case, asking what kind of
fish that was. And so they went from one to another,
and then to a different room.

6.

Suddenly Steven stopped. "Grandfather!"
He called loudly. "What kind of fish are these?"
"Those are seahorses," Grandfather answered.
"See, some of these are white and some are blue,
and some are red. Aren't they funny fish?"
"Yes," Steven agreed. "Look how they swim up and down.
They look just like little horses without legs."
He stepped up closer to the case.
"They are really funny fish!" He added. Grandfather laughed.
He could see that Steven was having a good time.
"Come!" He finally said. "Let's go on to the next one."

And so they went on to see many other
fish. They watched the lazy sharks slide through
the water. They saw the big octopus and
Grandfather counted its eight tentacles.
"The octopus is not a real fish,"
he told Steven,
"but it lives in the water like fish do."

After a while, Grandfather
looked at his watch.
"It's getting late, Steven," he said.
"I think we had better go home."
But Steven didn't answer. He was nowhere in sight.
"Oh my," Grandfather said.
"What could have happened to him?"
He tried to think of all the places
Steven might have gone.

He remembered how the big fat turtles
looked up and winked at Steven.
Maybe he's back there
watching them, he thought.
But when he got there, Steven was nowhere in sight.

10.

Maybe he's watching the Parrotfish, Grandfather thought.
But Steven wasn't there either.
Now he was getting very worried.
Grandfather looked and looked.
The big rooms of the aquarium began filling with people.
If I don't find him soon, Grandfather thought,
I'll have to wait until the aquarium closes
and then we'll be home too late for supper.

He saw a man in a blue uniform
standing near one of the cases.
That looks like a guard, Grandfather thought.
Maybe he's seen Steven?
He went up to the man. "Excuse me Sir.
Have you seen a little boy with blond hair?
He is wearing a sailor suit."

"Well, let me think," the guard said.
He took his hat off and rubbed his forehead.
"Yes, I guess I did.
A little boy asked me where the Seahorses were."

13.

"Of course!" Grandfather said to himself.
"Why didn't I think of that?
Thank you Sir," he said to the guard.
He turned and walked quickly to the
seahorse case. When he got there,
many people were standing around
and he couldn't see Steven.
He called out, "Steven!"

A little head poked out
through the crowd of people.
"Grandfather!" Steven was laughing.
Grandfather felt relieved that he had found Steven.
He was going to scold him for slipping away,
but changed his mind when he saw how happy he was.
"Come now," he said. "Let's go home."

Steven took one last look at the Seahorses.
Then he walked over to Grandfather
and reached up for his hand.
"This is a really special place," he said,
"and those Seahorses are the funniest fish
I have ever seen."
Grandfather was happy too. He took Steven's hand
and they left this very special place.

Turn the page to learn more about
the funny fish Steven saw on his adventure!

Glossary of Aquatic Life

Octopuses are sea animals known for their rounded bodies, large eyes, and 8 tentacles or "arms." These curious critters are playful animals that love to live in tropical waters. They will even find shells to make homes or use to play games.

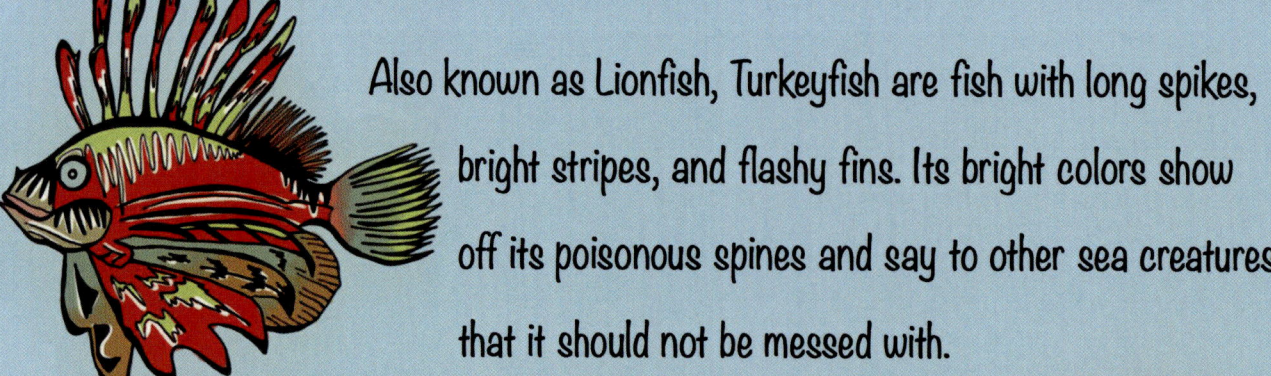

Sea Turtles are reptiles that spend most of their lives underwater swimming with their homes on their back. Every year Sea Turtles migrate, or swim to new places in the ocean and then back again.

Also known as Lionfish, Turkeyfish are fish with long spikes, bright stripes, and flashy fins. Its bright colors show off its poisonous spines and say to other sea creatures that it should not be messed with.

Although it says fish in their name, Jellyfish aren't actually fish! Instead they are sea animals that have jellylike bodies with no bones and slimy tentacles. Some types of Jellyfish are clear and small and some can be colorful and grow up to 6 feet long.

These colorful fish are named after their birdlike beak and large teeth. Whether they are sleeping in their slime pajamas, or scraping coral, these fish are always unique.

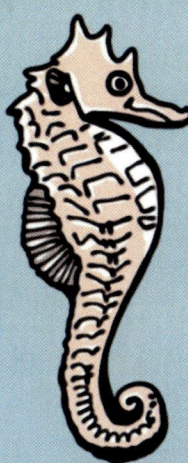

Seahorses are the slowest-moving fish in the sea. They are named for their unique shape, which looks like a horse! They even have a long tale that helps them curl and hold onto objects so they don't float away.

This type of fish is named for its long thin snout that looks like a sword. They are found all around the different oceans in the world like to swim in large open waters

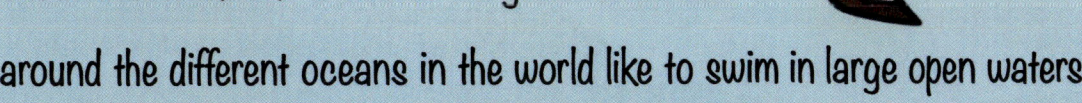

You may recognize this fish as "Nemo!" Clownfish are known for their stripes and for the bright anemones they live in. Their poisonous homes help defend them from other fish and keep them safe. In return, they help keep the anemone clean.

Sharks are fast swimming, large fish that have a skeleton made up of cartilage instead of bones! Sharks also have a sharp sense of smell up to 10,000 times better than humans.

About the Author

Ronald Semmann is a retired Wisconsin DNR officer, graduate of the University of Wisconsin- Madison, and co-founder of the Natural Resources Foundation of Wisconsin. He loves nature and spending time with his many grandchildren, but still finds time to write. His lifelong dream is to author and publish a children's book.
He hopes you enjoy the story.

About the Illustrator

Abbigail Semmann graduated from UW Madison in 2019 and now showcases her love for art as an art teacher.
She is one of Ronald's many grandchildren and is honored he chose her to illustrate his story. This is the first book she has illustrated and hopes to continue drawing in the future!